The Gold Prospector

The Gold Prospector

A Pan of Poems

Ginnie Cates

Illustrated by Amy Bond

To order additional copies of this book, contact:
Xlibris Corporation
0-800-644-6988
www.xlibrispublishing.co.uk
orders@xlibrispublishing.co.uk
300903

Contents

Dedication

For my parents Olive and Douglas who shared with me their love
of stories and poems when I was a child and taught me to
appreciate nature, creativity and contentment.

Foreword

Where experience pauses to wonder, the spirit of God breathes creativity. During these past months some of us have been entranced by the way that the Holy Spirit has been leading Ginnie on a journey deeper into God and into discovering herself. In one of the paradoxes of life, at the same time several actual longer journeys that she had planned to make have been cancelled for different reasons! The playful God revealed in some of these poems works his parables into our own experience.

Out of that experience can grow an enormous wealth of both inspiration and answer but it needs those who are bold enough to draw aside, to wait and to watch and to dare to love. Tentatively at first and then with increasing fervour Ginnie has taken the courage to stop, to look and to listen in simplicity. Initially through the harsh and fiery experiences of life and ultimately through being drawn deeper into the breathless reality of God's love and presence, what follows was born.

The prophets of our time help us to see what is so blindingly obvious that we wonder how we ever missed it. It is said that children smile and laugh four hundred times a day while adults do only fifteen. The reason often given is because no-one has taught children not to laugh. Jesus encourages us to be childlike as we embrace the Kingdom of God. Some of what follows helps us again to see life through childlike eyes so that again we smile with innocence. However, much harder to grasp is the fleeting whisper—what Elijah may have described as the "still small voice" of God. It is sometimes easy to read what follows too swiftly and think we have grasped the meaning and move on only to realise later that we have missed it. This is the other voice of the prophet—the message is there but we need to keep digging for it.

Woven through all the parables that follow is one larger narrative—that of the hand of God weaving the experiences together into something that is a rich and beautiful tapestry bringing the revelation of God in history into our own story. I hope you will enjoy, be encouraged and challenged by what follows. I also hope that this book will be the first of many and be an integral part of the mosaic through which God speaks today.

Rev. Graham Knott, Vicar, St. Mary's Church, Watford

Acknowledgements

Imagine coming home one day to find your wife in the throes of having a baby not your own. Over the course of the following days and weeks, her eyes bright with a new love, she is distracted, up at night and can't stop talking about it. Such befell my husband Chris and I would like to thank him for helping to foster and nurture this new life.

Then, from time to time, three grown up sons pop home to find the baby in residence. They too embrace her with brotherly affection, keep a watchful eye on her and even change the odd nappy. Thank you Matt, Pete and Si.

I am also blessed with a circle of friends who were as delighted as I was to see the baby born and grow. They made lots of encouraging noises which helped the baby learn to talk, tested the temperature of the bath water, and finally were entrusted with a pair of scissors to trim her exuberant hair. Thank you Angela, Jan, Janet, Joan and June.

The baby was fortunate enough to have Amy draw delightful pictures for her which made her smile and sing and to have her cot decorated with a beautiful cover made for her at Christchurch, Chorleywood.

Finally the baby had to listen to some bed-time stories which she didn't understand but which her mother enjoyed very much. These were the poems of TS Eliot and RS Thomas and three books: Preaching the Poetry of the Gospels (Elizabeth Michael Boyle); Word and Spirit at Play (Jean-Jacques Suurmond); and The Collage of God (Mark Oakley).

Poetic Licence

Poetic licence, sloppy grammar
Function dominating form
Stresses, syllables and metre
Shape how poetry is born.

Jostling words are armed for battle
Place and meaning, emphasis
Choices made while sabres rattle
Ideas (in parenthesis).

Image, metaphors and phrases
Drawn by dreaming earn their place
Some work hard to gain a mention
Others just slip in by grace.

Resonance is what we're after
That's it! Yes! Connection made!
Words that capture how we see things
Penny drops and light cascades.

Deep within emotions stirring
Paradox and truth align
Meaning from the dark emerging
Pattern recognition mine.

Poetry has helped me fathom
What was hidden, out of sight:
Oysters prised from sunless seabed
Pearls revealed reflect the light.

Know Answers?

Why d'you never see a baby
Pigeon, heron, stork or owl
Where are all their young selves hiding
Baby birds and fledgling fowl?

Why are white vans so aggressive
Why do buses brake so late
Why do drivers hog the mid-lane
Motorcyclists scorn their fate?

What's the hue of the equator
How long is a piece of string
Where's the brink from blue to yellow
Can you measure anything?

How much sun is there in music
Where do rainbows store their gold
When do stars begin their lunch break
Are you worth your wait when old?

I've a bookcase in my bedroom
Full of treasures I won't throw
At the top a shelf of wisdom
Lined with books called "I don't know".

Hello Mummy

Baby sitting in his buggy
Watching Mum with wondering eyes
Chatting, hoping, waiting, missing
Her attention, though he tries.

Mummy's plugged into her i-pod
While she's texting on the phone
Baby fiddles with his buttons
Finding he is all alone.

Child's Play

At six years old they view the world
In quite a different way
From grown ups who are prone to think
That they know how to play
Or how to let their hair down
At weekends, night or day.

The kids have found a better way
To see the earth and sky
Its funny side to make them laugh
In stitches till they cry
With hands and feet and actions
That begin to make them fly.

They do not need kaleidoscopes
Nor specs that see 3D
Nor bubble wands, binoculars
Inventions we might deem
A clever way to alter things
If you should wish to dream.

No, their way's much more fun than that
And simpler too and free
Available and portable
For hands and feet and knees
A topsy turvy way to play
As you will no doubt see

In parks and fields and gardens too
In swimming pools, on sand
On beaches, playgrounds, camping sites
And lawns throughout the land—
When upside down and back to front
They simply do handstands.

Field Road Junction[1]

There is a steam train near our home
The children love to see
The pressure builds to take them there
Whenever you are free.

Her engine's huge, her wheels are round
Her funnel belches steam
Her carriages are neat and smart
Her paintwork leafy green.

She rests upon a branching line
She's watered by the rain
Her crew are strangely absent
And she never takes the strain.

She doesn't travel anywhere
In fact she has no track
And yet she's still attractive
And the kids keep coming back.

There is a man who loves to keep
Her leaf-springs trim and flash
With tender care on bell and stack
Her shape cuts quite a dash.

She isn't made of metal though
She boasts no single rivet
Her cab is home to nesting birds
You see, she's clipped from privet.

No Breeze[2]

A sunny day beside a lake, its view obscured by trees
Except that is a tiny gap through which a baby sees
A sailing boat with bright pink sail, its occupant becalmed
Through lack of breeze or wind or gust, which leaves the baby charmed
To watch and wait and look and smile and notice that it's funny
To see a grown up stuck like that, frustrated, though it's sunny.
The baby has no need to rush, no targets to achieve
Content to wonder what it is that makes the grown-up peeved
On such a lovely sunny day with goslings, ducks and coots
Exploring by the water's edge her buggy and her boots.
The sailor meanwhile finds it hard to give up her agenda
Still, driven by the need to move, she longs for wind to send her
Across the lake and back to shore, the moment lost for ever
When just for once she might have owned the sea-change in the weather.

Rock, Paper, Scissors[3]

A children's hand game, quite well known
And played at school or in the home
That keeps them quietly amused
When bored in cars or stuck in queues.
It doesn't cost a thing to play
And who will win is hard to say
The young have just as much a chance
Of beating brothers, sisters, aunts,
As raising fists they count to three
Then swing them down for all to see.
The fun is in the quick surprise
To ascertain with smiling eyes
Who trumped that round, who conquered and
Who won the game by sleight of hand.
The scissors blunted by the rock
The paper by the scissors' shock
The rock defeated by the paper
A simple game, a jolly caper.
But grown-ups too have twice been shamed
By Federal Court and Art World named
To play the game as a solution
By which to find a resolution
When neither side could show the grace
To back down, keen to save their face.
And in God's world that's upside down
The wisest person is a clown.
The humblest sits upon a throne
The last in line is number one.
The outcome's not by us controlled
Nor are God's plans like dice unrolled
But those who seek him know his ways
Are best achieved through trusting grace.

Lullaby Flutterby[4]

At my arty smarty party
Busy Lizzie sang a song
Sitting on a sable table
'Where's my Curly Wurly gone?'

In the kitchen, beating, heating
Bakers caking with a spoon
In the oven, looking, cooking
Children needing feeding soon.

In the garden Wonky Donkey
Eating thistles by the stream
Lucky Ducky, Piggy Wiggy
Dipping in and out to dream.

Birdy Wordy singing sweetly
Gleaming, dreaming in the trees
Mountain fountain playing gently
Fluttering, uttering on the breeze.

In the meadows woolly jumpers
Fitter knitters, teasing yarn
Slower sowers, thinner spinners
Roly polies in the barn

Making certain curtains longer
Thicker knickers on the line
Scousers trousers, Hackets jackets
Airy fairies stitch in time.

Bedtime soon for cotty totties
Creeping up the stairs is best
Nestling in pyjamaramas
Hurly burlies laid to rest.

Visit to a Model Village[5]

On a sunny day in England
What could be a better treat
Than to visit such a treasure:
Every house and car and street
Shrunk in size to show a different
View of life, and one to suit
Plus a few anachronisms
Some anomalies to boot.

Walking gently through its pavements
Watching out for details fine:
Ice-creams melting in the sunshine
Village clock strikes half past nine.
Trains from different decades running
Through the tunnels black as pitch,
Stopping at the stations waiting
For the man to flick the switch.

Then emerging into daylight
Clicking-clacking through the fields
Vegetables and orchards growing
Valleys, hills and rolling wealds.
Children wonder at the zoo park
Sat in buggies that's until
They have spotted round the corner
Cable cars climb up the hill.

Man is running from a bull which
Chases him across the field
Heading straight into the train track
Something's going to have to yield!
Lady washing in her bedroom
Waving arms around her head
Maybe, though, she's cleaning windows
Wiping off their dirt instead?

Vintage cars at garage waiting
For repair from decades past
Sports cars, tourers, engines, tractors
Chassis that were made to last.
Couple kissing on the pavement
Paint pot falling through the air
Children spotting what is dropping
Lady needs to wash her hair.

Cricket match is now in full swing:
Size of ball is like a pea
Flying through the air and heading
Straight into a bonsai tree.
Village houses, shops and churches
Where the choirs sing out of tune
Congregation's praying, hoping
That the sermon's over soon.

Double-meanings in the signage
Bring a chuckle to the mums
Painter standing on the ladder
Balancing on highest rungs.
Rides are turning in the fairground
Miners digging out the coal
Hound dogs in the meadows chasing
Fox who's fleeing for his hole.

Suddenly a full size bumble
Lands upon the baker's tray
Buzzing on the cakes and biscuits
Wond'ring if there's jam today.
Children spotting in the distance
Fire emerging from the thatch
Smoke is rising from the cottage
Started by a careless match.

All of this is set in gardens
Beautiful with flowers and trees
Lawns with scissors neatly tended
Weeds the size of cars must be
Rooted out and swiftly banished
Lest illusion's quickly gone
Different size and scale confusing
Then the magic's soon undone.

Mother duck has made her home here
Ducklings—living, in her wake
Paddling in the village rivers
Unaware it's all a fake.
Wand'ring in and out of houses
Crossing roads without a care
Splashing in the ponds and gulleys
Pecking at the moving fair.

What a treat to spend a day here
All the world beneath our feet
Magic, memories and nostalgia
Is life quite so fair and neat?

Jersey's Quiet Day[6]

A friend who is a Yorkshire man
Says I can tell his tale
As Yorkshire folk like narratives
And this concerns a bale

Of hay, you may be wondering
Alone, or in a stack?
But this amusing tale took place
A week or two gone back.

Alone, in fact's the answer
To the question posed above
And in a field where farmer's hands
Had hauled and pushed and shoved

And placed the beneficial bale
(You may be wondering how)
Straight underneath a jersey-cross:
A disconcerted cow.

The cow was straddled in a field
Her partner looking round
Perplexed to see her neighbour stuck
With hooves above the ground.

With legs astride she stood quite still
Except, that is, her head
Which turned around occasionally
To drink or eat instead

From buckets which the farmer, kind
Had placed in front with care
To feed and comfort Jersey for
As long as she was there.

What was the point you might well ask
Of baling Jersey out?
The last straw for a restless cow
Uncomfortable, no doubt.

With tender joints and muscles sore
She had to take her ease
Tho' her natural inclination
Was to jump and bend her knees.

Now what, she asks with baleful eyes
Will be required for you
To grasp at straws which slip away
And contemplate the view?

Some God-inspired contraption
Which makes us hit the hay
To introduce some peace and quiet
And take the strain away?

A Summer Stroll

A summer stroll in heady June around the block, not field
The pavement radiating heat not far from Harrow Weald.
From gardens bright, the lime trees' scent is wafting all around
When suddenly from nowhere near some water hits the ground.
It splashes up my feet and arms and then straight in my eye
And looking up I scan the blue and strangely cloudless sky.
That's clearly not the source of this refreshing gentle shower
Which emanated now I see behind a lime tree's bower
A gardener sprinkler was the spring, its clicking I can hear
Invisible behind the hedge but clearly very near.
Instead of rushing on I stand and linger just a while
Appreciate its cooling touch and feel it raise a smile.

Summer Garden

Injured fledgling crow is walking
On the lawn, her right claw bent
Feathers ruffled, dipping in to
Pond, while magpies watch from fence.

In the ash tree baby squirrels
Acrobatic feats parade,
Froglets three are just emerging
From the pond in search of shade.

Butterfly and damsels hov'ring
In the sunlight, dancing free.
Nature in its early summer
Joyful, bright expectancy.

Now the magpie's turn to potter
Black and white with purple fleck
Grey dove's landed, sleek and handsome
Collar white around his neck.

Second magpie now is drinking
Then a third, while goldfish hide.
Spider on his web is resting
Insects flying to the side.

Each one of these lives is fragile
Nature's red in tooth and claw
But for now they've made it through
The portal of midsummer's door.

Charity bargains at home

Helping out in local high street
Volunteer for charity
Serving on the till or backroom
Quite a ragbag you can see.

Goods donated by the sackful
Everything from tat to new
Bearing quite a marked resemblance
To the bargain hunters too!

Rolex, Timex, clocks and watches
Metronomes in brown and black
Shoppers regular as clockwork
Same ones keep on coming back.

Sewing kits and knitting patterns
Balls of wool and potties too
Punters who delight to needle
Haggle, want to use the loo.

Works of Shakespeare, novels, comics
Candles, keys and washing lines
People who will take the Mickey
Out of prices, opening times.

Skipping ropes and tangled stockings
Scissors, pencil sharpeners, knives
Those who tie you up in knots then
Quickly cut you down to size.

Volunteers across the country
Donate hours both day and night
Those intent on bargain hunting
Could afford to be polite.

There are also many treasures
Strings of pearls and diamond rings
Those who smile, say please and thank you
Lift your spirits, make you sing.

So in shops across the country
Stocked with goods and bargains rife
You can see a microcosm
Best and worst of British life.

Affluence

Affluence contains a virus
Known as flu to you and me
Annual permutations mean it
Offers scant immunity.

Antidotes are largely absent
Laid up for a week or two
Weakened by the false assumptions
Put to bed when you have flu.

Much in life is easy pickings
Food and shelter for the rich
Health care, comfort, expectations
Life will pass without a glitch.

And that sense of independence
Back-up and security
Last, until the rug is taken
Wrenched from underneath your feet.

Life perhaps designed to show that
There is something to be learned
Rich and poor though rarely meeting
Both find one thing can't be earned:

All of us dependent on it
Hard work, effort can't bequeath
Though it's free it's also priceless:
Grace provides the air we breathe.

Building Blocks[7]

With what material today
Shall we begin to build, with hay?
There's plenty of it lying round
In fields and farmyards, on the ground.
Or what about some wood or straw
They're eco-friendly that's for sure.
And carbon neutral—with good reason
We can choose some crop in season.
What a good idea of ours:
Construction of an eco-house.
To choose organic makes such sense
And timber sourced for garden fence.

But there's a snag with wood and hay
They won't survive the fiery day
When all that we have built will face
The flames of judgment; then what trace
Of building will be left to see
Constructed out of straw or tree?
A house that's quick and cheap to build
May on that day no shelter yield.

The little piggies' tale is found
Within the bible's pages bound
Where silver, precious gems and gold
The heav'nly architect has told
Will on that day, revealed by fire
Withstand the flames of judgment pyre,
Because by nature they have been
Refined already, tested clean.
The dross removed, the searing heat
Has proved them wholly pure and meet
For building that will pass the test
Of entry to eternal rest.

But where to source such gems and gold?
In Revelation we are told
To buy them from the great Amen
The faithful witness, who in heaven
Is seated on His throne above
Preparing now a home of love.

The 12 Gems on Aaron's Breastplate[8]

The ruby red glow of the spilling sun
At the dawn of a perfect day

The radiant bright yellow of a daffodil
Where the lacewings and beetles play

The pale green whisper of Aurora's light
Dancing free in the starlit sky

The turquoise blue brilliance of a cloudless day
Where the lapwings and swallows fly

The bright blue green of the sunlit sea
Lapping shores made in paradise

An emerald green shaft locked in frozen flow
Through a glacier's pristine ice

The glistening wet flesh of a blood red orange
Split open on a china plate

The honey cream yellow in a bees wax cell
From a hive by the meadow gate

The vibrant rich purple of a violet flower
Singing brightly in a sunny dell

The yellow green skin of a Galia melon
Ripening slowly on the window sill

The narrow banded stripes of a favourite marble
Rolling round on a wooden floor

The glowing deep embers of a dying fire
Glimpsed at night through an open door.

Ruby, Topaz, Beryl, Turquoise, Sapphire, Emerald
Jacinth, Agate, Amethyst, Chrysolite, Onyx, Jasper

Who clipped her wings?

Who clipped her wings
And why?
And why were they afraid
She'd fly?
And who were they protecting
Her or them?
What has she missed?
What glories lay beyond
The clouds towards the sky
Where daydreams fly?

What dreams were lost
When scissors crossed
Cut through her quills?
To stay of course a host of ills.
Under the weather
Does she wonder whether
A feather can ever
Grow again?
She's learnt the answer
And it is 'No'.

A stunted, clipped one
Can't regrow.
The end of flight?
Not so.

For once the yearning has begun
To understand just what was done
And maybe why
A new set start to form.
The clipped ones are forlorn!
And on the wings of morn
The weeping done
New ones are born.

Young pinions rise
God's minions sigh
Opinions fly
And so does she ...

A Butterfly called Faith

How does faith appear to you?
As small, delicate and elusive as a butterfly?
But she can fly against a strong wind
And change direction
As fast as an arrow
Compared with her size.

Johari's Window[9]

Johari's window has four panes
You'll find him on the net
Four sections that can help you know
What you have seen and yet
It also helps you see what's still
Quite hidden from your eyes
It may be half of what you think
And quite a big surprise.

The top left square is what you know
You know, and under that
The bottom left is what you know
You don't know, that's a fact.
And what you don't know that you know
Is on the top and right
And under that's the killer
Always hidden from your sight.

This square is the important one
The bottom right of same
It's what you don't know you don't know
That causes all the pain.

On the Eve of Forever

You may believe He saw the stars
The sun, the moon, the night
The rainbow in the clouds above
The heavens full of light
But on the eve of that first day
Creation in the wings
He saw your twinkle in His eye
And heard the angels sing.

You may believe He saw the trees
The woods, the glades, the dells
The forests and the canopies
The oaks, the pines, the elms
But on the eve of that first day
Creation not yet neat
He saw the apple of his eye
Who made Him miss a beat.

You may believe He saw the hills
The mountains, Alps and Andes
The Himalayas, canyons, lakes
The Atlas and the Ganges
But on the eve of that first day
Creation on its way
He saw the peak of His desire
Who lifts His heart each day.

You may believe He saw the waves
The fish, the whales, the seas
The dolphins and Leviathan
The corals and the reefs.
But on the eve of that first day
Creation standing tall
He also saw your unformed love
The greatest catch of all.

Assumptions

I thought the moon was setting when I saw it late at night
It sat on the horizon and then disappeared from sight
But later on when I peered out to take another glance
I was surprised to see her half way through her stately dance
Across the sky, now beaming many moons from where she bowed
She clearly had not set but simply rose behind a cloud.
The opposite of what I thought had really taken place
The end had been confused with the beginning of a race
The waiting had been worth it and the second glance instead
Had proved how wrong assumptions can be turned upon their head.
The moon did not need raking from the pond or drawing down
But watching till she surfaced from behind her dressing gown.

The Gold Prospector

There lives a Gold Prospector
A kindly, gentle man
His ancient features yet belie
The ever youthful scan
Of searching eyes which eagerly
Are looking all the time
For gold He knows is buried deep
Within earth's treasure mine.

He isn't just Prospector,
He also owns the site
And gave to His beloved Son
The exploration rights.
But though He gave them freely
There was a cost to bear
A squatting tenant made it plain
He wasn't welcome there.

The tenant said "I'll fight for this—
Evicted I am not.
There's plenty I can tempt Him with
And make Him lose the plot."
The desert was the chosen place
They squared up for a duel
The tenant tanked up for a fight
The Son was short on fuel.

"You're starving are You? Never mind!
I've heard You've got the power
To turn these rocky stones to bread
So prove your loaf this hour!"
But when he failed a second time
He tried a different tack
"If You will only worship me
I'll give Your kingdom back".

The sitting tenant then withdrew
He knew he'd lost that fight
But he'd be back before too long
And this time in the night.
A garden was the setting now
The desert having failed
He upped the stakes of evil power
But Sweat and Blood prevailed.

The Son now weakened faced a night
Of onslaught, violent scorn
But bruised and battered by the fight
Survived to face the dawn.
The final test was on the cross
The squatting tenant jeered
"Why don't you call for back-up?"
While death and evil sneered.

And then, the end. The tenant smiled
Then laughed and rubbed his hands
His rights assured, his rule intact
Surveyed his subject lands.
The earthquake and the darkness black
The curtain ripped in two
Did worry him a little bit
Beyond his power, he knew.

And then his haunting fears increased
And slew him one by one
Another earthquake followed by
The Resurrected Son!
The Son's rights now reclaimed and sure
Are writ and sealed in blood
His ownership now guaranteed
Has opened up a flood:

His prospect streams are beckoning
To pan for precious gold
His rocks pulsate with silvered veins
His heart with joy untold.
X marks the spot where rubies hide
The cross has shown the way
The Treasure Seeker's swelling chest
Is filled with pride today.

With love in mind, pure joy in heart
And treasure map in hand
He searches out his priceless pearls
And jewels throughout the land.
The Gold Prospector with His Son
And Spirit dancing round
Rejoice to hear the happy clunk
Of spade on treasure-ground.

Colour Swatch?

Walking off to work one morning
Bumped into my neighbour Jim
Bottles—three—of milk he's holding:
Red-top, blue-top, semi-skimmed.
Told, when asked him for the reason:
"Got the decorator in!"

Lord! I'm expecting

Lord, your timing's awful!
I'm busy, can't you see?
And making preparations
For Your nativity!

Our relatives are coming
The angel outfit's made
The turkey is defrosting
The Christmas cards displayed

The snow spray's on the window
The Asda slot is booked
The fairy lights are working
The Christmas pudding's cooked

The shepherds' tea towels gathered
The Christmas parties done
The carol singing's finished
The midnight service sung

I've wrapped up all the presents
And iced the Christmas cake
Baked mince pies by the dozen
I'm tired, for goodness sake!

And now, last straw, this letter
A civic census called!
It's sixty miles to travel
And frankly I'm appalled!

Somehow my expectations
And yours have all got crossed
I don't know if you've thought this through
And factored in the cost

I've done all you have asked me
Was thrilled to be the one
The virgin you had chosen
To incarnate your Son

I dreamed of royal cot sheets
Of purple, red and gold
But everything's gone pear shaped
My apple pie's gone cold

And now I'm on this donkey
My dreams all might-have-been
I hoped you would have ordered
A stretch pink limousine

My Braxton Hicks have started
The birthing pool's not booked
I'm feeling cross and anxious
There's much you've overlooked

No mother to assist me
No midwife there to say
Push now, breathe deep, well done love
What use are cows and hay?

I loved the wooden cradle
That Joseph carved with care
I wish that I was able
To lay my baby there

But looking in His shining eyes
Contentment beyond measure
'A sword will pierce your own soul too'
But pain gives birth to Treasure.

The Love Traveller's Bride

From time immemorial
Comes love eternal
To woo his beloved
Earth ephemeral

The Quest

'Twas New Year's Eve and thick with snow
Outside, a howling gale
A medieval banquet hall
The setting for this tale.

A Prince stood up with gentle face
A young but level head
A starlit twinkle in his eye
And this is what he said:

"Before the king, my father, died
He made this one wish known:
That I should search for wisdom's gift
Before I take the throne.

But winter's not the time for quests
The forest's thick with snow
Three knights I'll need, the first may plan
And in the spring he'll go".

The peasants gathered round the Prince
And marvelled at his plans
To search for wisdom's priceless jewel
From kings of distant lands.

The spring arrived and with its warmth
The birds began to sing
The forest oaks began to bud
The castle bells to ring.

The first knight of the chosen three
Was summoned then and told
"The king you find must be bequeathed
This sceptre made of gold".

The knight set off, the sceptre fine
Was to his saddle sewn
His one particular request,
That he should seek a throne.

He galloped off and journeyed long
Through fields and rivers wide
By forests, mountains, hills and plains
And then one day he spied

A peasant girl with royal crest
Embroidered on her shawl
He followed her and found himself
Inside a royal hall.

And there he saw the royal throne
Amazement in his eyes
This surely is the place he thought
To educate the wise.

He thanked the king and left his gift
And headed back for home
Of all he'd witnessed in that court
He marvelled at the throne.

He couldn't wait to tell the Prince
And peasants what he'd heard
But he was asked to hold his tongue
And not to breathe a word.

Then summer came and with it flowers
That made the senses reel
The second knight was summoned
And bequeathed a sword of steel.

"Your task, once you have found the king:
To try and glimpse his steed
Then offer him this sword of truth."
The knight knelt and agreed.

He too set off on charger proud
The sword in scabbard placed
And cantered on by sunlit woods
Through fields his hoofsteps traced.

And then one day on far off hill
A distant stable spied
He slowly climbed the bridle path
Exhausted by the ride.

But once inside the building dark
He glimpsed the royal steed
His charger reared to see the horse
An awesome sight indeed.

He placed beside the royal mount
The scabbard and the sword
Then led his horse by rivers deep
And splashed through stream and ford.

He too was sworn to silence by
The Prince who welcomed him
And then one misty autumn morn
The third knight summoned in:

"Now, you must take this yoke of bronze
And seek the royal bed
To glimpse the sovereign's resting place
And lay it near his head".

The knight set off and soon he found
The chamber that he sought
And gently stepped across the boards
To place the gift he'd brought.

He too was shocked by what he saw
But reaching in his sack
He found the burnished yoke of bronze
And placed it round his back.

The journey home took many weeks
And so 'twas Christmas Eve
Before the Prince could summon all
The knights, their tale to weave.

The snow fell silently outside
The tots had gone to bed
The knights stood up to tell their tale
And this is what they said:

"The king's throne is a bouncy chair
His bed: a travel cot
The sovereign steed: a rocking horse
He's just a tiny tot!"

The Prince stood up and thanked the knights
For hearing wisdom's call
"A life-time's insight I have gained
With which to serve you all".

The Legacy

With a splinter removed from my foot
I trod gently with steps that were light
Not because it continued to hurt
But because I just felt that it might.

Office Chair

Sitting on an office chair
Gas inside to smooth the op
Picking up a catalogue
Was enough to make it drop.

The Master Perfumer

There lives a Master Perfumer
The skilful, cheery Nez[10]
His rosy plan from dawn of time
To make fine fragrances

Just one, in fact, his heart's desire
A signature divine
Distilled from three essential oils
He planned to call it "Mine".

He laboured in his factory
Collecting nature's scents
Fine tinctures from creation's still
The best ingredients.

Creation, tainted, swerved to rot
But then he found The One
Solution—Spirit—Self-expressed
The Essence of his Son.

He breathed their triple accent notes
Base, heart and head, all three
Inspired the rich and heavenly scent
A perfect symphony.

The heart-shaped bottle made of glass
He polished till it shone
The fragrance, ruby red in hue
The Master's heart had won.

To keep it safe was not his plan
The scent—a gift divine
Etched on the glass in royal font
A label: "This is Mine"

Thus, formed of clear and fragile glass
Susceptible to danger
He reached through frosty starlit skies
And placed it in a manger.

Discovered by a peasant girl
She shouted "Oh my Word!"
And recognised its worth at once
Its scent to barn preferred!

She valued it and kept it safe
Unique and special treasure;
The smell got right up Herod's nose
Though, causing great displeasure.

He sent his guards to sniff it out
They traced it to a village
And, armed with mallets, pick and axe
Began to smash and pillage.

The peasant girl escaped with 'Mine'
To desert country, fast,
Where incognito she could live
Until the threat had passed.

Returning home she wore the scent
For thirty years or more
Its everlasting fragrance meant
No trips to perfume store!

Its scent had spread throughout the land
Its properties sublime
Had made both friends and enemies
The former won, in time.

The perfume-makers in the land
Felt business under threat
They smashed the glass to smithereens
Those wearing "Mine" just wept.

The friends picked up the broken shards
And placed them in a box
The enemies wound up the case
With chains secured by locks.

For three days, grief and sadness, then
A miracle took place!
The shattered glass reformed by fire
Burst right out of its case!

If you would wear this perfume fine
You'll need to change your skin
Combined, the two enable you
To love the skin you're in.

When washed, new skin absorbs the scent
Aroma worn with pride
A splendid, rich anointing oil
Bouquet for heaven's bride.

Calm Down

Calm down
Settle up
Come down
Rise up

Play down
Work up
Lay down
Fork up

Slow down
Speed up
Fall down
Stand up

Let down
Make up
Hunker down
Snuggle up

Write down
Type up

Eyes Right

Funny thing, I've got some floaters
Hundreds of them, in my eye,
After vitreous detachment
Debris just keeps floating by.

I can see it's there, though oddly
Looking from the outside in
Nothing's changed, my eye looks normal
Not the way it is within.

Floaters here to stay the surgeon
Says, remaining in my eyes
Not to worry though, as in a
Year, your eyes 'habitualise'

Brain adjusts to foreign objects
In effect says they're not there.
Floating planks I'm now quite used to
Look as if they've disappeared.

Optician

I went to the Optician
A two-fold problem raised
My distance vision blurry
And close-up vision glazed.

He asked me lots of questions
Did line and letter tests
Discussed a range of options
The lenses he thought best.

I looked at varifocals
Their colour, style and frames
My eyebrow raised at prices
Of smart designer names.

I booked the next appointment
And focussed on the day
When all would be much clearer
A week or two away.

On entering the clinic
He showed the specs to me
Imagine my amazement
When both of them were free!

He gave me my prescriptions
The distance pair called 'Faith'
And etched upon the close up lens
'The hidden depth of Grace'

Dance of the Giants

The Father of the universe and galaxies sublime
The black holes, stars and nebulas receding back in time
Gave birth one day in history to his celestial Sun
Whose blazing, searing, molten heat gives life to only One.
The centre of the Milky Way attracting planets nine—
The Earth alone is flourishing, a treasured, special sign.
And She was graced a Play-mate in the gentle, silver Moon
Whose Spirit hides then dances round and plays a wistful tune.
A Trinity of friendship, when the Father, Spirit, Sun
Invited Earth to share with them their laughter, love and fun.

Hide and Seek

The moon which disappeared last month has turned up in the sky
In quite a different place from where I thought, I wonder why
Her path I find so hard to trace, the route she takes to track
When just as I begin to get the hang of her she's back
Confusing me, she starts to point her horns the other way
And equally she's happy shining through the night or day.
The sun's chart on the other hand's more subtle, even plain
He doesn't ply so many where's but plays a different game.
Between the two of them it seems a picture may be seen
A golden orb is circled by a silver robing queen.
Perhaps they are companions who engaged upon a dance
Between them hear the music to conduct a fine romance.

Sign of Affection[11]

The sunlight plays
The heavens tune
The constellations blink.
The planets turn
The black holes bend
The light, and Venus winks.

The moonbeams dance
Auroras dawn
The red dwarfs play high jinks.
The thunder claps
The lightning strikes
The ground and Venus winks.

The cloudburst breaks
The showers fall
The black and white clouds link
The grey skies brush
The rainbow paints
Her ribbons—Venus winks.

Sonnets[12]

A single soapy bubble left the bath
A thousand foaming others stayed behind
And upwards, gently rising, traced its path
Towards the ceiling high its heart inclined.
Reflected in the sphere a window frame
Two images were seen, both upside down
Of summer garden trees within the pane
Refracted in the coloured rainbow gown.
Upwards it rose and kissed the ceiling white
And lingered for a while its home to know
Then, satisfied, began its downward flight
And felt the pull of gravity below.
Alighting, gently, in the foam immersed
And one by one the bubbles all dispersed.

99

The locals thought him odd and crossed the street
He rummaged through the bins and dressed in rags
With holey loafers on his blistered feet
His tattered sleeves were stuffed with plastic bags.
He wasn't always seen to take bits out
He often used to put bobs back as well
And sitting on the pavement used to tout
For free exchange of what he'd found to sell.
One night a youth resolved to follow him
And down an alley dark began to stride
When all at once he saw a disused gym
With party lights and laughter bright inside.
Hung on the door a sign read "Welcome All"
And peering in he saw a banquet hall.

999

The blacksmith struck the final blow then stood
Admiring in his forge the work of art
The furnace stoked with stacks of crackling wood
The red hot flames had seared the molten heart.
Before him on the bench a weather vane
The arrow and the anvil pointing east
And singing sweetly by the window pane
A little bird on crumbs was pleased to feast.
The vane, complete with heart, was sold and placed
High on a windswept barn one winter's morn
Exhausted soon because it always traced
Its path towards the east where it was born.
One day the little bird flew down and said:
'Go with the wind and rest a while instead'.

9V

A windmill and a water wheel both worked
In fields of corn where rushing water streamed
On facing sides where neither of them shirked
The chance to grind the flour the farmer gleaned.
Ignoring one another, both denied
A single common purpose jointly owned,
On airless days the mill, exhausted sighed
In summer drought the water wheel just groaned.
And then one day a spider spun a thread
Between the mill and wheel across the race
And webbing back and forth it simply said
"You'll both wear out if you maintain this pace"
The breathless air and water made no sound
And heard the sail and wheel stop rushing round.

V

A comic incident occurred today[13]
Banana cake was rising in my mind
A recipe had seen the light of day
Extracted from the bookcase, lost behind.
A bunch of five sat by the window pane
O'er ripened by the radiant summer heat
The yellow skin had ceded black terrain
I picked them up by stalk to make the treat.
When all at once they started to unpeel
All five of them beginning from the top
The skins removed themselves, as they could feel
The pull of gravity and would not stop.
I tried to catch them falling—two or more
The rest, now peeled, just landed on the floor.

V9

A dungeon bare, dressed with a veil of fear
The chains, the bars, the walls, all thick as thieves
The air hung low with portraits of despair
And in the window, framed, a young man grieves.
The rent unpaid, his life is torn apart
A double crime when he was forced to beg,
While dreaming of his baby breaks his heart
His tattered clothes reveal his broken leg.
And then one day, no crutches left to burn
His cell walls shivering, his fever rife
A stranger comes with aid he couldn't earn
And freely offers him the key to life.
Attached, the crucial "Paid" stamped on the bill
And bread and wine upon the window sill.

V99

The door, just like the cross, was made of wood
The heart, just like the tomb, was cut from stone
The door, impregnable, a lifetime stood
And yet contained a window to its home:
Kaleidoscope of bright and coloured glass
Through which the light of life would daily play
And dance in hallway, singing as it passed
Through portal round, a springtime world displayed.
A bolt, a key, a chain were all in place
And rusty hinges spun with cobwebs free
And then one day a voice which sang with grace
Knocked on that door and waited patiently.
The Visitor was holding a receipt
On opening up the heart began to beat.

V999

An ancient fishing harbour, brisk with trade
A seasoned fisherman, the night's work done
And on his stall a thousand fish displayed
Their silvered rainbow edges catch the sun.
With fair exchange of talents, luck and skill
The bartered fish and money both change hands
With hungry birds attracted by the krill
A squawking, flapping seagull roughly lands.
The fish and money scatter on the ground
A coin worth four nights work rolls in the sea
But soon the lure by watching carp is found
Whose glint he swallows all expectantly.
Unfed, the carp a parable enacts
As from its mouth he pays the temple tax.[14]

𝒢𝒞

He placed it on the path, a stumbling-stone
Deliberate act, designed to make them fall
The road was broad and millions walked alone
As one by one they each were forced to stall.
They stubbed their toes and tripped and grazed their knees
'Twas night, and all were taken by surprise
But up ahead a cliff face no-one sees
And just in front the road forks: life or lies.
The warning felt, two keys each turn a lock
As morning breaks they all brush off the dirt
And curse the one who placed the stumbling-block
And made pride's air bag fill and egos hurt.
But some have stood upon the cross-shaped stone
And glimpsed an unlocked gate and distant throne.[15]

H

He stood on planks inside the disused well
Two hundred feet above, the same below
He'd seen three nights and days pass since he fell
His cries for help had nowhere left to go.
With slimy walls no purchase could be found
No steps or rungs by which he could escape
The only way was down towards the ground
The end would be decisive, make or break.
He prayed and leapt and then began to glide
And landed in the empty pit below
And there he saw a door was open wide
And this time there was somewhere left to go.
The door led to a second living well
And up above he heard a shepherd's bell.

XV

A diving helmet, enigmatic sight[16]
Magnificent in size and shape and form
Of burnished gold and copper panels bright
An image fit for eve of heaven's dawn
Is lifted up and placed upon a roof
Of apex shape with tiles of slated grey
And in the helmet's radiant splendid truth
A solar panel nestles night and day.
But how did such a diving helmet breathe
Before the days of cylinders attached
For divers searching out the watery deep
From pearl or wreck or coral craft despatched?
A breathing tube was lowered from on high
Inflating lungs which gasped for sight of sky.

XII

Her name was Mary, and she brought four things:
Her tears, her hair, an alabaster jar
The jar contained a pint of purest nard
The fourth thing that she brought—a life of sin
To Jesus who reclined in Simon's house
A Pharisee, a leper, sharing food
She stood behind Him, quiet as a mouse
And then the tears began and formed a flood.
They poured down on His feet and made them wet
She dried them gently with her hair and yet
Twas not enough, she broke the jar and then
She poured the perfume on the Son of Man:
At first His head, His body, then His feet
Until the fragrant offering was complete:

XLIX

The perfume sweet soon filled the leper's room
Anointing oil worth one year's wage or more
Harsh words of pious judgment followed soon
Self righteous hatred oozed from every pore.
"Leave her alone!" The Christ rebuked them all
"Her act shows pure devotion, loving touch
Her sins were many, now she loves as much
As she has been forgiven, warts and all.
You did not kiss my cheek when I came in
You did not give me water for my feet
Nor bless my head with oil or perfume sweet
Her actions show she's overwhelmed by sin.
Her faith has saved her, she may go in peace
Her story, like her fragrance, is released".[17]

XIV

The lovely voice stood calling from the hills
Through sunlit valley streams it made its way
The singing breeze brought whispers from its rills
To where a maiden fair was wont to lay.
A longing deep within began to stir
To listen to that voice and come away
And driven by the breeze which called to her
She journeyed over many a night and day.
The whisp'ring voice was waiting her embrace
And sang with tender notes of heav'nly love
Delight and beauty brought them face to face
And wedding bells were heard in heaven above.
The bride and bridegroom kissed in perfect peace
And entered hand in hand the wedding feast.

The Silence of God

The silence of God
Is not the absence of noise
But the presence of stillness
Followed by a smile

End Notes

1. Field Road Junction
   This lovely life-size hedge in our village is maintained by the owner Richard. As it is half way between the local park and our home it provides a good resting place for little legs which are tired walking between the two.

2. This poem is seen through the eyes of baby Miriam who was taken to the Rickmansworth Aquadrome by two of her great-aunts, June and Ginnie when she was 9 months old.

3. In 2006 a Federal Judge in Florida ordered two sides in a lengthy court case to settle a trivial point using the game of rock, paper, scissors. The game was also used to choose which one of two auction houses would receive the rights to auction millions of dollars worth of impressionist paintings.
   (Wikipedia.org)

4. Lullaby Flutterby
   In English poetry the rhyme usually falls on the last syllable of the line. This poem is an attempt to rhyme on the penultimate syllable as is common in the Romantic languages. As it happens I found it more satisfying in this poem to rhyme on both the penultimate and ultimate syllables but within the same line.

5. Visit to a Model Village
   One of my favourite holiday activities. This one is in Buckinghamshire.

6. Jersey's Quiet Day
   As I mention in the poem, a true story witnessed by a friend of ours.

7. In the bible: 1 Corinthians 3:10-15

8. The 12 Gems on Aaron's Breastplate
    A description of the breastplate with its twelve gemstones and its function can be found in the bible in Exodus 28:15ff.

9. Johari's window takes it name from Joseph Lugt and Harry Ingham who in 1955 in the United States used this cognitive psychological tool to help people better understand themselves and how they relate to others. Charles Handy later developed the idea to include four rooms or windows. Room 1 is the part of ourselves that we see and others see. Room 2 is the aspect that others see but we are not aware of. Room 3 is our private space which we keep from others. Room 4 is that which is in our subconscious which is seen neither by us nor others. (Wikipedia.org)
    This poem attempts a simple explanation of the theory.

10. Nez: A friendly name for a Master Perfumer, from the French for 'Nose'.

11. Sign of Affection
    This poem may make some wonder about 'possessive punctuation', e.g. should the word 'heavens' in the second line have an apostrophe? The question cannot really be answered one way or the other because the poem deliberately includes several double meanings whereby the object of one line becomes the subject of the next.

12. A Sonnet—technically speaking:
    The Shakespeare Sonnet has just fourteen lines
    A rhyme scheme formed of just AB, AB
    CD, CD, EF, EF assigned—
    And at the end a couplet you will see.
    The word means little song or little sound
    Each line contains ten syllables, no more.
    The meter by iambic pentams ground
    Tee tum tee tum yet makes the poem soar.
    The ninth line of Petrarchan marks the spot
    The flip or volta where the problem turns
    To resolution of the well-wrought plot
    The end is where the current reader learns:
    The sonnet style is here above rehearsed—
    My first attempt to write in such a verse.

13. This is difficult to imagine but as I was holding the over-ripe bunch of bananas by the stalk the skins of all five split at the base of the stalk and started to unpeel in unison and quite beautifully. Three landed on the floor without their skins and had to be discarded but I managed to catch the other two which had also unpeeled spontaneously!

14. The last line of this sonnet makes a biblical reference which is found in Matthew 17:24-27.

15. This sonnet makes several biblical references, two of which are found in Romans 9:33 and Matthew 7:13.

16. This picture suddenly came to my mind when I was wide awake and was so striking I wanted to write about it.

17. These two sonnets draw on two stories in the bible found in Matthew 26:7; Mark 14:9; Luke 7:32 and John 12:3.

Lightning Source UK Ltd.
Milton Keynes UK
01 November 2010

162231UK00002B/32/P